DO THE MUSLIMS HAVE AN ARGUMENT?

PETER G. R. MAC RAE, MA

COPYRIGHT

2017

TABLE OF CONTENTS

PAGE

PREFACE

Do the Muslims have a valid argument for today's troubles and violence in the Muslim world? Do Muslim "*Extremists*" have a valid argument for their acts of violence against the West and against fellow Muslims? Is the West blameless, or is the West responsible in whole or in part? All parties share in the responsibility. However, do the ends justify the means?

"If you cannot argue the other side's position intelligently, you will likely lose on your side." This was my caution to my fellow graduate students and the undergraduates for whom I was the teaching assistant in upper division courses in International Conflict Resolution. My fellow graduate students and the professors in our Political Science department labelled me "the token Conservative", to which I would reply, "If all of you had been arguing the Conservative side, I would have argued the Liberal." While I have strong views on the subject matter, with this in mind, I will attempt to make this paper as objective as possible. Applying the principles of International Law as they pertain to the events presented, the reader will be able to come to their own conclusions.

This paper will be in six chapters:

1. The Muslim responsibility for their current position.

2. The West's historical treatment of the Muslims.

3. The descriptions of concepts in International Law.

4. The justifications for or against Muslim violence.

5. The West's justifications for or against its current reaction.

6. The ongoing questions.

SECTION ONE

THE MUSLIM RESPONSIBILITY FOR THEIR CURRENT POSITION

When one finds that they have fallen from the pinnacle of power and influence to the near bottom, as has happened to a good deal of the Muslim world, who do you blame? "Who, or what, caused this to happen to us?" Human nature is such that one searches for scapegoats. It is difficult to accept total responsibility for one's misfortune and humiliation. [1]

Muhammad ibn Abdullah, also called Ahmad, (circa 571-632) [2] founded Islam in the late sixth century, whereupon he became known as Prophet Muhammad. Islam rapidly gained wide appeal. It provided order and rules to what had been theretofore nothing but warring Arab tribes. Islam put in place an ordered and simple life. By the fifteenth century the Islamic world was the most powerful force on earth. Islam spread out of the Middle East from what is now Saudi Arabia and stretched from the Atlantic Coast of Africa, through the Iberian Peninsula and as far east as present day Indonesia. To be sure, not everyone came to the faith willingly. Large portions of the lands controlled by the Muslims were conquered by their Islamic armies.

It was a faith of culture and learning. The Muslims gave the world the concept of zero. Though invented in India, we have the Muslims to thank for Arabic numerals. (Try adding, subtracting, multiplying and dividing in Roman numerals.) The Muslims developed the concept that the day is divided into twenty-four equal hours.

As difficult as it may be for some to believe, the Koran preached a tolerance for other faiths. For example, in the lands that the Muslims conquered, Jews and Christians were allowed to worship freely, so long as they paid the tax which the Muslims imposed.

Early on the flaws began to emerge. Islam divided into two sects, the Sunnis and the Shiites. Today nearly ninety percent of all Muslims are Sunnis. The Sunnis recognize the first four caliphs, or rulers, who ruled in accordance with the Koran and the Sunna. The Sunna refers to the teachings and practices of Muhammad. Further, Sunnis believe that Muhammad did not appoint a successor but that the successors should be those who are the most competent and chosen by the community. On the other hand, after Muhammad's death, the Shiites recognized the first Imam (first Believer of the faith) as Imam Ali, Muhammad's cousin and brother-in-law. They believe that all successors must be Imams of the household and descendants of Muhammad and that they alone have the right to rule. In short, the Sunnis believe that the most capable Imams should be the successors. The Shiite believe that Muhammed's successors must be linked by heredity. That is the main schism which has created the violent intra-faith conflict that is present today. In fairness, the same was true within Christianity. One has only to look at the Inquisition, the birth of Protestantism and the bloody conflicts with Catholicism. The difference is, while there are many Christian sects, Christianity has largely put the violent confrontations behind it. Not so within Islam.

Bernard Lewis, in his book *What Went Wrong*, emphasizes 1) the Muslim's distain for the West and 2) the Muslim subjugation of women (3) as some of the reasons for the Muslim decline. Lewis also points out that some observers advocate that the Muslim decline had more to do with the rapid advances in the Western World than to a Muslim decline. San Diego State University Political Science professor, Dr. Dipak Gupta, in a 2003 lecture, cited four causes that contributed to the downfall of Islam from the most powerful force on earth to today's diminished condition. Those four causes include: 1) the refusal to develop *Inductive Reasoning* to accompany *Deductive Reasoning*; 2) no interest in the West; 3) no navy, and 4) the discrimination of women (Gupta, 2003). Briefly, an

explanation of each of these four causes follows:

1. *The refusal to develop Inductive Reasoning to accompany*

Deductive Reasoning. Islam never embraced the concept of *Inductive*

Reasoning which is reasoning by observation. Inductive Reasoning means

that *truth*, but not absolute proof, can only be ascertained by the

examination of the evidence. Therefore, according to Inductive

Reasoning, all hypotheses are subject to challenge. It is an approach from

the *specific* to the *general*. That is, an observation (the specific) is made.

Next, one looks for other like patterns. This is followed by a tentative

hypothesis. Finally, a theory (the general) is developed. While the West

embraced Inductive Reasoning, Islam held fast to *Deductive Reasoning*

which is reasoning by set rules or laws which dictate that the conclusion is

certain. That is just the opposite of Inductive Reasoning in which the

conclusion is *probable*. As an over simplification, an example of

Deductive Reasoning begins with a concept (the general) and moves

through a hypothesis which looks for patterns which support the

hypothesis which then leads to the *certainty* of a *specific* example. "All

dogs have long ears. Fido is a dog. Therefore, Fido has long ears."

2. *Islam had no interest in the West.* Islam is not a state. However, with the same assuredness of any conquering state, the Muslims, during the course of their rise, had nothing but contempt for Europe. They considered the people to be barbaric. Cold Northern and Western Europe held nothing of interest to the Muslims. Conversely, by the early part of the Age of Discovery, nearly every state in Europe had within their academia a school of Asian Studies. The Muslims had no such studies with respect to Europe. In fact, up until that time Islam had only translated one European book, a French work which was a treatise on syphilis (Lewis, 2002). That contempt for Europe became a hate with the invasions of the Holy Land by European Crusaders beginning in 1096. This was even though the Muslims generally prevailed over the Crusaders until the Muslims ultimate expulsion from the Iberian Peninsula. The Granada War of 1482 to January, 1492 waged against the Muslims by Ferdinand and Isabella resulted in that expulsion from Spain with the signing of the Treaty of Granada in 1491, (4) and finally from Portugal in 1496. To this day the grudge is still there. To the Muslims the word *"crusaders"* is a derisive word. In today's conflicts with the West we will often hear the Muslims referring to the West as the (Invading) Crusaders.

3. *No navy.* The Muslims never developed a navy in the Western sense. They felt no need. They controlled the land trade routes

throughout their sphere of influence. They believed that any threat to their empire would come by land, not by sea. They considered their biggest threats as coming from Asia or the Russian Steppes. Unfortunately, Vasco de Gama sailed around the Horn of Africa in 1497 and on to India demonstrating that seafaring commerce with Asia was very feasible. During the Age of Discovery, states such as England, France, Holland, Spain and Portugal were sailing out, discovering new worlds, colonizing, vastly increasing their wealth and knowledge, and becoming more and more powerful as they defended their winnings.

What should have been a major wake-up call was ignored by the Muslim world. The New World and Asia supplied Europe with much of the raw materials that they had once imported from the Middle East, such as coffee, sugar and spices. Now Europe was exporting these same products to the Muslim world! The Muslim world was nearly rendered redundant insofar as trade between Europe, Asia and South Asia was concerned. The Muslim world was being left behind in an economic surge. During this era, the trading posts and ports developed by the European powers in Asia became their dependent colonies which were not just confined to the coast but extended far into the interior.

4. *The discrimination of women.* The fourth of the causes cited by both Bernard Lewis and Professor Gupta was, and is, the Muslim

discrimination and suppression of women. This discrimination caused many of the Islamic states to deprive themselves, then and now, of a great source of intellectual power. One could argue that a full fifty percent of their population is deprived of being added to the Islamic world's intellectual body. The few gains that have been made by Muslim women have produced physicians, lawyers, engineers and teachers. That is a testament of what could have been, or could be.

So when did the decline begin? Some may argue it began with the expulsion of the Muslim Moors from the Iberian Peninsula in the fifteenth century. From the twelfth to the fifteenth century the battles for power, including the Crusades, raged.

In the later part of the seventeenth century the Muslim Ottoman Turks battled a coalition of European Christians, the Holy League, for control of much of Eastern Europe including Vienna, Poland and Ukraine. The Holy League, which was blessed by the Pope, was joined by Russia. The Ottomans lost. The Muslims lost a considerable amount of territory. With the Treaty of Carlowitz in 1699 the Muslims learned some bitter lessons. The most important of which was the realization that they had to deal with the outside world and had to develop diplomacy and a willingness to negotiate. This, with a civilization that they had heretofore dismissed as barbaric and of no use, was a medicine not easily swallowed.

The battles and the losses continued. In the eighteenth century they warred with Russia and in 1774 the Ottoman Turks lost the Crimea. That loss was devastating in that the Muslims considered that territory as part of the heart of their homeland.

There was a painful realization. The Muslims needed the Infidel: Infidel teachers, Muslim students! The Muslim world turned to the European world for arms, modern supplies and training. What makes it particularly painful is this need was, and is, satisfied by a culture and a religion that for over a thousand years the Muslims have despised. European cultures and religions had been considered to have nothing of value except as a source of slaves and converts to Islam.

The slide continued. As the West grew more powerful and outstripped the Muslim world in technology and production, the Muslims could not compete. Beginning with the sixteenth century the Western powers began colonizing much of the Third World and Islam found itself in servitude to the West.

The hatred born of colonization cannot be minimized. Much of the bitterness of being dependent territories of European states may well be justified. As a side note, we must remember that unlike Great Britain and

France, the United States did not have colonies in the Muslim world.

Salifi is an Islamic word. It means a pure life according to the faith, a simple, devout life. For many Muslims the fall is God's punishment for Islam and its believers having strayed from the true path. That straying from the true path, according to many Muslims, is the result of *Creeping Westernization.*

It is the view of many of the Fundamentalist mullahs that Western culture, values, materialism and the Western push for more democratic institutions and women's rights in the Muslim world are undermining Islam. Mullahs are Islamic "teachers" similar to Christian preachers. In this age of technology, information travels universally and instantly. As the people of the Muslim world see the perks of Western living they have become desirous. Those Muslims who, for example, have access to the Internet want the clothes, music, computers, entertainment and freedoms they witness on the Internet. Many Muslim women no longer cover themselves. Many wear Western clothes. In some Islamic states the young are particularly influenced by Western materialism and values. The mullahs blame all of this on the West. So, for many of the mullahs, Islam is in a struggle, a "*jihad*", to save their religion and culture.

It appears that, in large part, the Muslim world having fallen behind the advancements of the Western world is the result of cultural,

religious norms and tactical errors. To that degree, the West probably

should not be blamed. There are, however, legitimate justifications for the

Muslim resentments of the West.

THE WEST'S HISTORICAL TREATMENT OF THE MUSLIMS

There were conflicts with the West before the eleventh century, such as the conquest by the Muslims of the Iberian Peninsula. For the purposes of this paper we can begin with the Crusades. It is not the mission of this paper to give a history lesson on the Crusades. However, the reader should be cautioned. In the literature, there are many conflicting accounts as to the causes for, and the blame for, the Crusades.

The Crusades were a series of major campaigns from the end of the eleventh century to the end of the thirteenth century. For example, the first Crusade lasted 1096 to 1099, the second from 1147 to 1149, the third from 1189 to 1192, the fourth from 1198 to 1229 and minor battles continued until the end of the thirteenth century.(5)

So, how did they begin? In 1095 the Byzantine Empire was in trouble. The Byzantine Empire, also known as the Eastern Roman Empire lasted for over a thousand years until it fell to the Ottoman Turks in 1453. From the fourth to the sixth century the Roman Empire's eastern Greek and western Latin split. Constantine made Constantinople the Byzantine capital and Christianity became the official religion. In the twelfth century Constantinople was the largest and wealthiest city in Europe. The

Byzantine lands went through several periods of decline and recovery. At its height it controlled the Western Mediterranean, North Africa, Italy including Rome and provinces in Egypt and Syria. Those two provinces were lost to the Arabs.

The Muslim Turks had seized control of Byzantine holdings in Asia Minor, and they were threatening Constantinople. Alexis Comnenus, the Byzantine emperor, wanted to regain lost territory so he sent a plea for help to Pope Urban II. Pope Urban II had far greater ambitions than just aiding Comnenus. Pope Urban II saw a fight employing large groups of Christians fighting for the "glory of God" and increasing the authority of the Church. Additionally, Pope Urban II's incentive was to bring the Greek Orthodox Christians in the East under the control of the Roman Catholic Church in the West, thereby expanding his power. His power had been challenged in the West by lay nobility and particularly Holy Roman Emperor Henry IV who had driven Pope Urban II from Italy to France. (6)

Pope Urban II's call to arms for the first Crusades was given in a speech to clergy in the French town of Clermont wherein he called upon the French to "rescue" Jerusalem from the hands of the infidel, as he referred to the Muslims. He hinted at the possibility of creating new kingdoms in the Holy Land. He vastly exaggerated the threat of the annihilation of Christendom at the hands of the Muslims. He accused the Muslims of atrocities against Christians. His claims were largely false. Islam, in reality, was tolerant of other faiths. Pope Urban II offered protection for the property and families of those who would join the Crusade. Pope Urban II promised that all who went would have all their sins forgiven and upon death would go directly to Heaven. (7)

According to a paper titled "The Dark History of the Knights Templar", (8) crusader Raymond of Aguiles boasts of incredible cruelty. He recounts decapitations, torture and burnings by the Crusaders. This account is documented by Desmond Seward in his book, *The Monks of War*. (9) Seward asserts that in July, 1096 Jerusalem was sacked. "The entire population of the Holy City was put to the sword, Jews as well as Moslims (sic). 70,000 men, women and children perished….men waded in blood up to their ankles". Desmond states that another historical source put the number of Muslim deaths at 40,000. The literature does point to European motives for land, trade opportunities and plunder. It is alleged that the Crusaders disemboweled their victims under the theory they had swallowed their gold and jewels. (10)

Those atrocities resembles the atrocities committed today by al

Qaeda, the Taliban, Boko Haram and ISIS. However, the atrocities attributed to the Crusaders are disputed by Thomas F. Madden, "The Real History of the Crusades". (11) Madden claims the Crusades were "in every way defensive wars". According to Madden they were a response to Muslim aggression and conquests of Christian lands.

The Crusades battles waged on, effectively ending in 1229 with back and forth defeats and victories for both the Muslims and the Crusaders. Additional conflicts continued, culminating in the expulsion of the Muslims from the Iberian Peninsula. Other territorial losses were highlighted above in the Section One.

From the 1600's onward it is no secret that the European powers consisting of England, France, Spain, Portugal, the Netherlands, Russia and Germany considered the world their property. Each founded colonies to promote trade, often without any regard for the local citizenry. In the late fifteenth century Spain and Portugal negotiated an agreement dividing the world between themselves. That division was sanctified with the Treaty of Tordesillas in 1494. (12)

Slavery was a big part of the trade. Approximately sixty percent of all the slaves acquired by the Europeans came from Muslim territories in North Africa. Possibly twenty per cent of the slaves shipped to the

Americas from the Muslim areas of Africa were Muslims. (13) There is little question that both the Europeans and the Muslims took slaves during their frequent battles. However, from a Muslim point of view today, only the European taking of Muslim slaves is relevant to them.

The Ottoman Empire was a Muslim empire, and it existed from the thirteenth to the first two decades of the twentieth century. At the height of its power it controlled much of North Africa, the Iberian Peninsula, the Middle East and parts of Arabia. Beginning in the sixteenth and seventeenth century the Ottoman power began to wane as they lost battles with the Europeans. In fairness to the Europeans, some of the lands the Ottomans had conquered were considered by Christians as holy. From there the Europeans, led by England, France and to a lesser extent, Spain, Portugal, Italy, the Dutch and the Russians, set about gradually taking control of nearly all the territories once claimed by the Ottoman Empire. (14)

Initially, the Europeans were primarily interested in trade. They established trading colonies in North Africa, the Middle East, and India became an English colony. The Europeans recognized the value of controlling these areas. With Ottoman acquiescence, which the Ottomans too late realized, European commercialism grew as a result of economic expansion and the European attempts at control of language, culture and political penetration. (15)

The British East India Company used an army and employed force to protect their interest in India and pushed north into Muslim Afghanistan to buffer against Russian incursions from the north. According to Adam Ritscher, "During this time, on two separate occasions (which became known as the Anglo-Afghan Wars), British armies from India outright invaded Afghanistan in attempts to install puppet governments amenable to British economic interests and that would oppose the economic interests of Czarist Russia." (16)

The first, which became known as the First Anglo-Afghan War, took place in 1838. Outraged by the presence of a single Russian diplomat in Kabul, the British demanded that Afghanistan shun any contact with Russia or Iran, and that it hand over vast tracts of Pashtun inhabited land to British India (regions that are today part of Pakistan). Dost Mohammad, the Afghan ruler, agreed to these humiliating demands. Nevertheless, the British still invaded the country. The British seized most of the major cities in Afghanistan with little resistance, but their heavy handed rule soon resulted in a popular uprising by the people which resulted in the massacre of the entire British army of 15,000, save one. (17)

In 1858 the British claimed sovereignty over India. There were more incursions. The British became involved in conflicts in the Arabian Peninsula and established a military outpost in Oman.

Napoleon invaded Egypt in 1798 but withdrew in 1801. Later the French did occupy parts of North Africa. (18) Through propaganda, Napoleon's attempts to convince Egyptians that they were victims of imperial oppression, presumably Ottoman, was unsuccessful. However, beginning in the early nineteenth century, Christian subjects of the Ottomans in the Balkans did begin to feel victimized by Ottoman rule. This phenomenon was likely influenced by the Balkan Christians exposure to European ideas through contacts and education. The Europeans fed these feelings of oppression by encouraging local wars. The Balkan Christians were attempting to gain freedoms and independent states. The anti-imperialism movement against the Ottomans gained momentum in Anatolia and gradually spread among Arab nationalists after 1900. (19)

Again, Ritscher: "British outrage over the uninvited arrival of a Russian diplomatic envoy in Kabul in 1878 resulted in the Second Anglo-Afghan War. Again the British were able to occupy all of the major cities, but unlike on the previous occasion, the British got wind of an impending rebellion against their occupation, and brutally crushed it in a preemptive move. They did subsequently withdraw, but not before they set up a puppet ruler and forced the country to hand over control of its foreign affairs to Britain.......” Afghanistan would remain a British protectorate until 1919. (20)

European imperialism took on three significant dimensions in the early part of the nineteenth century: 1) Direct occupation and colonization; 2) diplomatic pressure on the Ottomans for economic and legal privileges, and 3) treaties to control seaports in the Persian Gulf. In the second half of the nineteenth century the Ottomans granted concessions to build canals, railroads, telegraph lines and banking operations. The Ottomans sought loans from the Europeans, and when they were unable to meet their debts, the Europeans assumed control. Anti-European imperialism, as a reaction to the growing number of concessions, resulted in the Tobacco Revolt in Iran in 1891. (21)

World War I bought with it an interesting set of historical facts with respect to the European treatment of the Muslim world. For our purposes, British and French actions are of primary importance.

An unassuming young Briton found himself the champion of a downtrodden people in the middle of events that changed the course of history. His name was T. E. Lawrence. He first went to the Middle East as part of a scientific exploration. As a result of his subsequent exploits he became known as Lawrence of Arabia.

The discussion, with respect to Lawrence of Arabia is based on an article in the Smithsonian Magazine article, "World War 1: 100 Years Later, The True Story of Lawrence of Arabia". (22)

Prior to World War I, for his history thesis, Lawrence traveled to Syria to study the Crusader castles of Syria. Subsequently, he joined an archeological expedition. In Syria, Lawrence developed a clear, if simplistic, view of the Ottoman Empire. He admired the free-spirited Arab and was disgusted by the corruption and inefficiency of their Turkish overseers. Lawrence championed the idea of the Arabs being free of Ottoman imperialism. The opportunity, and the chance for Lawrence to play a role, arrived when Turkey entered the war on the side of Germany and Austria-Hungary. Because of his experience in the region, Lawrence was dispatched to Egypt which was the British base of operations for the upcoming campaign against the Turks. He was promoted to the rank of second lieutenant in military intelligence.

Lawrence had studied the clan and tribal structure of Arab society. He intuitively grasped the delicate negotiating process necessary to win tribal leaders over to the rebel cause. Waging war in early 20th-century Arabia revolved around the primary issues of where an army on the move might find water and forage for its animals. Very quickly Faisal, the third son of Emir Hussein, ruler of the Hejaz region of central Arabia, came to regard the young British officer as one of his most trusted advisers. Lawrence assumed a position of honor in tribal strategy sessions.

After protracted secret negotiations with British authorities in Cairo, the British promised Emir Hussein a recognized Arab kingdom. In June of 1916 Hussein then launched an Arab revolt against the Turks. With British naval help, the Arabs captured a succession of Turkish-held towns along the Red Sea coast. Initially matters had gone well. Catching the Turks by surprise, Hussein's rebels seized the holy city of Mecca along with Jeddah, but there the rebellion stalled. By October of 1916, the Turks remained in firm control of the Arabian interior, including the city of Medina, and appeared poised to crush the rebels. When Lawrence learned that a friend in Cairo was being dispatched to Arabia to gauge the crisis, he arranged a temporary leave from his desk job to tag along.

It was over the course of that ten-day visit that Lawrence had managed to fully entrench himself in the Arab rebel cause, and to win the confidence of Faisal. In short order, Lawrence was appointed the British

Army's temporary liaison to Faisal, a posting that soon became permanent.

In September 1917, Lawrence and his Arab followers attacked a troop train just south of the Ottoman garrison in Mudowarra, Jordan, destroying a locomotive and killing some 70 Turkish soldiers. Mudowarra, the southernmost town in Jordan, was once connected to the outside world by means of the Hejaz Railway. The Hejaz Railway was an attempt by the Ottoman sultan to propel his empire into modernity and knit together his far-flung realm. By 1914, the only remaining gap in the line was located in the mountains of southern Turkey. Had that tunneling work been finished, it would have been theoretically possible to travel from the Ottoman capital of Constantinople all the way to the Arabian city of Medina, 1,800 miles distant.

Instead, the Hejaz Railway fell victim to World War I. For nearly two years, British demolition teams, working with their Arab rebel allies, methodically attacked its bridges and isolated depots. The British and the Arab rebels realized that the railroad was the Achilles' heel of the Ottoman enemy. It was the supply line linking the Ottoman's isolated garrisons to the Turkish heartland. Lawrence personally blew up 79 bridges along the railway, becoming so adept that he perfected a technique of leaving a bridge "scientifically shattered", ruined but still standing. Turkish crews had the time-consuming task of dismantling the wreckage before repairs could begin. By war's end, damage to the railway was so extensive that much of it was abandoned.

Based on the promises made to the Arabs, Hussein's son Faisal and Lawrence marched into Damascus at the conclusion of World War I to set up an independent Arab state with Faisal as leader. Unfortunately, Lawrence also harbored a guilty secret. From his time in Cairo, Lawrence was aware of the extravagant promises the British government had made to Emir Hussein in order to raise the Arab Revolt: full independence for virtually the entire Arab world. What Lawrence also knew was that just months after cementing that deal with Hussein, Britain had entered into a secret compact with its chief ally in the war, France. Under the Sykes-Picot Agreement, the future independent Arab nation was to be relegated to the wastelands of Arabia, while all the regions of value, meaning Iraq and greater Syria, were to be allocated to the imperial spheres of Britain and France. Even though conscience-stricken, Lawrence recruited ever more tribes to the cause of future Arab independence.

Originally the Sykes-Picot Agreement was to include Russia. However, during the Russia revolution the Bolsheviks discovered the agreement, causing the agreement to be publically exposed. Nonetheless, the Conference at San Remo formally cemented the division of the Arab world between Britain and France. Even though Mark Sykes and Francois Georges-Picot intended the new states to conform to local customs and traditions, it was not to be. With the now straight lines demarcating states, the British and French did not seriously consider ethnic, cultural or even the religious differences between the populous. When Faisel opposed France, the French sent in troops to expel him from Damascus. Subsequently, the British established him as the leader of the newly formed state of Iraq under British control. (23)

The Sykes-Picot Agreement and the 1920 Conference at San Remo greatly diminished the Arab dreams of fully independent Arab states at the conclusion of World War I. The terms of those two agreements may well have contributed significantly to today's conflicts in the region. (24)

By the beginning of the twentieth century Britain and France recognized the strategic importance of oil. Oil was a major driving force as to how the British and the French administered their newly "mandated protectorates" in the Middle East. The mandates were sanctified by the League of Nations at the conclusion of World War I. For example, the British set up the Anglo Persian Oil Company in which the British

Admiralty was the major shareholder. The lion's share of the oil accrued

to the British. (25) Over the course of the first half of the twentieth century

several nations got a share of the oil spoils of war. This included Russia

and the United States. In 1946, the British subsequently excluded Russia.

Prior to World War I, during the reign of the Ottoman Empire, the

modern states of Iraq and Iran were known respectively as Mesopotamia

and Persia. The modern states of Iraq and Iran were British creations. In

1925 the British installed Reza Shah Pahlavi ruler of Iran. He was

deposed in 1941 and replaced by his son, Mohammad Reza Pahlavi, who

was either controlled by, influenced by, or pressured by the British, with

American assistance, until the 1979 revolution (26) which led to the

expulsion of Shah. Suffice to say that the British effectively installed and

controlled the governments of both Iran and Iraq.

How does the creation of Israel fit into the picture? The story

begins with the Alfred Dreyfus Affair which started in 1894. French

Army Captain, Alfred Dreyfus, of Alsatian and Jewish descent, was

accused and convicted of treason and given a life sentence. He allegedly

committed espionage by giving French military secrets to the German

Embassy. However, in 1896 new evidence pointed to the guilt of French

Army Major Ferdinand Esterhazy. In a subsequent two day trial,

Esterhazy was acquitted. More charges were brought against Dreyfus with a new prison term. Dreyfus was eventually pardoned and restored to the Army with the rank of major. His convictions were believed to be a miscarriage of justice based, to a large extent, on anti-Semitism. The affair convinced the European Jews that, in order to be safe, they must have a state of their own. (27)

On November 2, 1917 a letter was written by British Foreign Secretary Arthur James Balfour to Lord Lionel Walter Rothschild, head of the British Zionist Federation. It became known as the Balfour Declaration. (28) It reflected the October 31, 1917 decision of the British Cabinet for an "act of policy" supporting a Jewish homeland.

The Balfour Declaration was the result of pressure from the Jewish community in Great Britain. The declaration was the outgrowth of years of negotiations following the French Dreyfus Affair.

The Balfour Declaration merits reproducing in full:

Foreign Office
November 2nd, 1917

Dear Lord Rothschild,

I have much pleasure in conveying to you, on behalf of His Majesty's Government, the following declaration of sympathy with Jewish Zionist aspirations which has been submitted to, and approved by, the Cabinet.

His Majesty's Government view with favour the establishment in Palestine of a national home for the Jewish people, and will use their best endeavours to facilitate the achievement of this object, it being clearly understood that nothing shall be done which may prejudice the civil and religious rights of existing non-Jewish communities in Palestine, or the rights and political status enjoyed by Jews in any other country.

I should be grateful if you would bring this declaration to the knowledge of the Zionist Federation.

Yours sincerely,
Arthur James Balfour (29)

The language of the British government was vague on the subject of a specific homeland so the Jewish Zionist interpreted the policy as a Jewish state in Palestine. At the same time, the Palestinians and the Arabs interpreted the policy as insuring their rights. (30) The League of Nations entrusted Great Britain with the Palestine Mandate.

According to Pierre Tristan, in his article, "What Is The Balfour Declaration?" he states, "At the time of the Declaration in 1917, Palestinians—the 'non-Jewish communities in Palestine'—constituted 90 percent of the population there. Jews numbered about 50,000. By 1947,

on the eve of Israel's declaration of independence, Jews numbered

600,000. By then Jews were developing extensive quasi-governmental

institutions while provoking increasing resistance from Palestinians.

Palestinians staged small uprisings in 1920, 1921, 1929 and 1933, and a

major uprising, called the Palestine Arab Revolt, from 1936 to 1939. They

were all quashed by a combination of British and, beginning in the 1930s,

Jewish forces" (31)

In 1939 an attempt was made to ease Palestinian and Arab

resistance with the British unilaterally issuing a "White Paper". The paper

called for the establishment of a Jewish national home within an

independent Palestinian state within 10 years. It did not call for an

immediate Jewish state or the possibility of partitioning Palestine. Jewish

immigration was to be limited to 75,000 for 5 years. Any further Jewish

immigration was to be at the discretion of the Arab majority. The rights

of Jews to buy land from Arabs carried restrictions. It also promised that

only with Palestinian support would Britain allow a Jewish state. This

greatly upset Zionists and they rejected the White Paper. The White Paper

was accepted by the Arab Higher Committee. A campaign of Jewish

attacks on government property and Arab civilians lasted for several months. On May 18, 1939 a Jewish general strike was called. While the White Paper was official British government policy until 1945, its primary provisions were never put in effect. (32) Israel declared its independence on May 15, 1948. The Balfour Declaration was Israel's foundation.

At the end of World War II, the United States emerged as the world's "super power". Most of the world looked upon the United States as their protector. It became a role that the United States, rightfully or wrongfully, accepted. At the same time, under the rule of Josef Stalin, the Soviet Union was increasing its power. The USSR, a totalitarian state, made no secret about their ambition to spread Communism throughout the world. This condition was abhorrent to Western values. The United States led the "Free World" in checking Soviet ambitions. Thus, the Cold War with its accompanying "Arms Race" was on.

There is a saying, "The enemy of my enemy is my friend". Following this philosophy, the United States supported, propped up, helped bring down or helped install regimes around the world. In many cases they were regimes resented by the local citizenry. Nevertheless, the United States supported those regimes solely on the basis that they were opposed to Communism. This included governments in the Middle East.

The United States receives a minimum of its oil supplies from the Middle East. Certainly, it is much less than Europe's dependency on Middle East oil. However, oil is possibly one of the most important commodities in the world. So much so that President Dwight Eisenhower declared oil a "strategic commodity" worth fighting for. That has driven much of the United States foreign policy, particularly in the Middle East. Therefore, by inserting itself in the affairs of foreign states and actions to insure the supplies of oil, the United States has caused deep resentments in the Middle East.

At the end of World War I, Great Britain had offered to share the territories they now controlled from the defeated Ottoman Empire. With respect to the United States, President Woodrow Wilson declined. However, under Harry Truman, the United States began its involvement. America was instrumental in forcing the Soviet Army out of Iran immediately after World War II. However, under Truman the United States solidified America's relationship with Mohammed Reza Shah Pahlavi, in power in Iran since 1941. Then, in 1953 Eisenhower ordered the CIA to depose Mohammed Mossadegh, the popular, elected leader of the Iranian parliament and an ardent nationalist who opposed British and American influence in Iran. The coup severely tarnished America's reputation among Iranians, who lost trust in American claims of protecting democracy. (33)

In 1947 the United Nations, which had been conceived at the end of World War II, initiated a plan to partition Palestine. The plan proposed granting 57 percent of the land to Israel and 43 percent to Palestine. Truman personally lobbied for its success. The plan lost support from United Nations member states, especially as hostilities between Jews and Palestinians multiplied in 1948, and Arabs lost more land or fled. Truman recognized the State of Israel 11 minutes after its creation, on May 14, 1948. (34)

Two more policy positions and actions are noteworthy. 1) During the 1980s, the Reagan Administration supported Israel's expansion of Jewish settlements in occupied territories. 2) The administration also supported Saddam Hussein in the eight-year Iran-Iraq War. The administration provided logistical and intelligence support, believing that Saddam could destabilize the Iranian regime and defeat the Islamic Revolution. (35)

The United States has been successful in mediating some disputes between the Israelis, the Palestinians and other Middle Eastern states. The

United States has dispensed foreign aid to nearly all the actors. However, it is clear that the United States is Israel's ally. The United States has so stated on numerous occasions. This policy position has exacerbated the animosity of the Muslim world against the United States.

SECTION TWO

THE DEFINITIONS OF CONCEPTS IN INTERNATIONAL

LAW

Before we begin an analysis of the events surrounding the 2001/2002 invasion of Afghanistan and the 2003 invasion of Iraq, a few descriptions may be in order.

International Law struggles with the definitions of genocide, crimes against humanity, what constitutes torture and most of the other terms describing international conflict. Therefore, it is left to individual states or responsible organizations to interpret and evaluate these acts. Typically, they will do so in a manner that suits their purpose. The terms are: (1) *Genocide*, (2) *Crimes against Humanity*, (3) *Aggression*, (4) *Sovereignty*, (5) *Responsibilities of Sovereignty*, (6) the *Piercing of Sovereignty*, (7) *Intervention*, (8) the *Just Wars Doctrine*, (9) *Responsibility to Protect*, (10) *Right of Self-defense* and (11) *Preemptive Strikes* are terms that are difficult to precisely define. Therefore, it appears that the best we can do here is review the literature in an attempt to describe the characteristics of each of the terms.

When analyzing the justifications of the combatants in the next two sections, these following reviews may serve as the criteria for assessment. This paper will not attempt to resolve these issues, rather it will attempt to explain how they relate to the current conflicts.

Genocide

If we look to the United Nations Charter for a definition of *Genocide*, we will be hard pressed to find one. The only mention in the Charter that could even come close would be in Chapter XI, "Non-Self Governing Territories," wherein Article 73 refers to "just treatment" and "protection against abuse." Nowhere in the Charter is genocide addressed specifically. Given the atrocities of World War II, this is a curious omission. However, it should be noted that the United Nations Charter does allow for reference to other conventions and other human rights treaties. (36)

The Genocide Convention of 1948 defines genocide in Article II. It does so by listing the acts that are intended to destroy, in whole or in part, a national, ethnic, racial or religious group. Those acts include killing, serious bodily or mental harm, conditions calculated to bring about physical destruction, preventing births, and the forcible transfer of children (United Nations Office of the High Commissioner for Human Rights 1948). (37) With respect to parties charged with acts of genocide, the Convention refers to them as "persons charged." Does "persons charged" expressly include any governmental, including an entire government, or non-governmental group? Presumably it does.

Crimes Against Humanity

Article 7 of the Rome Statute of the International Criminal Court characterizes *Crimes Against Humanity*. "For the purpose of this statute, 'crimes against humanity' means any of the following acts when committed as part of a widespread or systematic attack directed against any civilian population, with the knowledge of the attack: (a) Murder; (b) Extermination; (c) Enslavement; (d) Deportation or forcible transfer of population; (e) Imprisonment or otherwise severe deprivation of physical liberty in violation of fundamental rules of International Law; (f) Torture; (g) Rape, sexual slavery, enforced prostitution, forced pregnancy, enforced sterilization, or any other form or sexual violence of comparable gravity; (h) Persecution against any identifiable group or collectivity on political, racial, national, ethnic, cultural, religious, gender as defined in paragraph 3, or other grounds that are universally recognized as impermissible under

International Law, in connection with any act referred to in this paragraph or any crime within the jurisdiction of the Court; (i) Enforced disappearance of persons; (j) The crime of apartheid; (k) Other inhumane acts of a similar character intentionally causing great suffering, or serious injury to body or to mental or physical health." (38)

Aggression

International institutions struggle with respect to a definition of aggression. The United Nations General Assembly adopted a deliberately incomplete definition with its resolution 3314 of December 14, 1974. The Statute of the International Criminal Court (ICC) provides for the crime of aggression but the ICC has stipulated that it will only "exercise jurisdiction" after a definition has been adopted through an amendment to its charter.

The Charter of the United Nations treatment of aggression is seriously deficient. The issue of aggression is addressed only five times in the entire Charter and in some of those instances one must infer aggression. They are so few that they can be highlighted as follows: (39)

1. Preamble: "…that armed force shall not be used, save in the common interest…"

2. Chapter I, Article 1.1: "…suppression of acts of aggression or other breaches of the peace…"

3. Chapter I, Article 2.4: "All Members shall refrain in their international relations from the threat or use of force against the territorial integrity or political independence of any state…"

4. Chapter VII, Article 39: "The Security Council shall determine the existence of any threat to the peace, breach of the peace, or act of aggression…"

5. Chapter VIII, Article 53.1: "…renewal of aggressive policy on the part of any such state]…"

One could surmise that the Charter's position on aggression is that no state should initiate violence upon another state (Article 2.4) and that such acts of aggression are contrary to International Law.

However, the lack of definitive enforcement rules against aggression often creates endless debate, and therefore, causes states to interpret aggression as suits their national interest. The above stated

Article 2.4 is as close as the Charter comes to being definitive on the issue of aggression.

Perhaps, in an attempt to prohibit aggression as law, the United Nations could borrow from Quincy Wright. Writing earlier in 1935, Wright proposed that, "A state which is under an obligation not to resort to force, which is employing force against another state, and which refuses to accept an armistice proposed in accordance with a procedure which it has accepted to implement its no-force obligation, is an aggressor, and may be subjected to preventive, deterrent remedial measures by other states bound by that obligation". (40)

Antonio Cassese (2001) makes an excellent observation: "It would be fallacious to hold the view that, since no general agreement has been reached in the world community on an exhaustive definition of aggression, perpetrators of this crime may not be prosecuted and punished". This statement makes two important points: (1) That perpetrators may be prosecuted, and (2) the problem of ambiguity. (41) Cassese charges that the problem with aggression was that the major Powers preferred to avoid defining this breach of the ban on force laid down in Article 2.4 of the United Nations Charter, so as to retain as much leeway as possible in the application of that provision.

Sovereignty

In today's world, the issue of *Sovereignty* becomes more complex and critical from a world safety perspective. What events cause a state's government to jeopardize its sovereignty, in whole or in part, through acts of unconventional aggression? Could these include the increasing problems of terrorism, genocide, the broad scope of human rights violations, and civil conflict? Could they also include states' direct or indirect support of those acts?

"What then is sovereignty? To say that a state is sovereign means that it decides for itself how to cope with its internal and external problems, including whether or not to seek assistance from others." (42) This quote of Kenneth Waltz is by no means a definition of sovereignty; rather, it is a description of one of the features of sovereignty. It is germane to this discussion because it gets to the heart of the issue of the rights of the international community, or lack thereof, to intervene in the affairs of states. This is important with respect to aggression and its potential effect on the international community.

The United Nations Charter sanctifies the notion of state's sovereignty. It does so in Article 2.1 which states, "The Organization is based on the principle of the sovereign equality of all its Members."

Article 2.4 goes on by stating in part, "All Members shall refrain in their international relations from the threat or use of force against the territorial integrity or political independence of any state…." Sub-paragraph Seven (Art. 2.7) is even more direct, "Nothing contained in the present Charter shall authorize the United Nations to intervene in matters which are essentially within the domestic jurisdiction of any state…."

Article 2.1 sets the stage. It declares that the United Nations is founded on the idea of the sovereign equality of all its members. It is the declaration of a principle or a general guide. Unfortunately, states are left to interpret these Articles as suits their national interests. Additionally, in times of crisis these insufficiencies often create endless debate resulting in inappropriate action, delayed action, or no action.

Responsibility of Sovereignty

Do states have *Responsibilities of Sovereignty* or are they able to treat their citizens and the outside world with impunity? International Law is beginning to recognize that sovereignty carries responsibilities. However, there does not appear to be succinct criteria for the abrogation of sovereignty rights. In fact, there are competing views. Grotius said that, "…all states, in their dealings with one another, are bound by the rules and institutions of the society they form. They are bound not only by rules of prudence or expediency but also by imperatives of morality and law". (43)

Vattel, in his work, *The Law of Nations*, states that, "...the law of nations

is the science of the rights which exist between states, and the obligations

corresponding to these rights". (44)

The Piercing of Sovereignty

The *Piercing of Sovereignty* is closely linked to the

Responsibilities of Sovereignty. Under traditional International Law,

states could very well do as they pleased, including aggressively

intervening in the internal affairs of other states. (45) That would imply

that the sanctity of sovereignty was reserved for the powerful and that

sanctity is somewhat tenuous for the not so powerful. The United Nations

Charter attempts to mitigate the ability of the powerful to aggressively

intervene in the affairs of the not so powerful with respect for the

sovereignty of those states in Article 2.4. It also makes this attempt by

appointing itself as the sole determiner of a breach of the peace in Article

39 and as the sole authority for the use of force in Article 42.

Former United Nations Secretary General Javier Perez de Cuellar

stated, "I have no doubt that a major challenge for the U[nited] N[ations]

in the future will be to find the right balance in the desperate situations

that will arise between respecting sovereignty and maintaining peace and the security of mankind. The view has become increasingly accepted that

the principle of nonintervention in matters that are within the domestic

jurisdiction of states cannot be regarded as a protective barrier behind

which human rights can be systematically violated with impunity." (46)

Intervention

With respect to *Intervention*, it was noted above that in traditional

common law, states could do essentially as they pleased including waging

aggressive war. That is no longer the case. However, the common law

issue of intervention is mixed. There are those who posit that any

intervention is always illegal. Third World states are the foremost

proponents of this view. Others believe that, under certain circumstances,

intervention is justified. During the 1990s, a majority of the international

community came to regard the relief of human suffering and protection of

human rights as legitimate causes for *Military Intervention*. In fact,

military intervention often is a necessary tactic for stopping the internal

conflicts that are so harmful to attaining these goals. (47) (Lahneman

2004b). (48) The most likely proponents of this position are those who

subscribe to the Responsibilities of Sovereignty.

Current International Law primarily vests the power of authorizing

interventions with the Security Council of the United Nations. Article 2.3

directs states to settle their disputes by peaceful means. Article 2.4 admonishes states not to use force or to threaten to use force in the settlement of disputes, and Article 2.7 prohibits the use of force in interventions which are essentially within the domestic jurisdiction of a given state. Article 41 of the Charter spells out the preferred methods of intervention, namely sanctions and/or the severance of diplomatic relations. Article 42 grants the Security Council the exclusive power to authorize the use of force. The only exception in the United Nations Charter to the prohibition of the use of force is found in Article 51 of the Charter, the *Right of Self-defense*. Even then, the party defending itself must report immediately to the Security Council and cease action as soon as the Security Council "…has taken measures necessary to maintain international peace and security…."

It is important to note that all of the references in the Charter to the use or non-use of force are directed to state-to-state conflict. No specific rules can be found with respect to today's typical conflicts such as terrorism, genocide, and civil conflict.

Since the 1990s, the United Nations has taken a greater interest in intervention in domestic and human rights issues. In the 1990s, the Security Council showed greater creativity in defining such threats. (49)

However, Michael Glennon is scathing in his assessment that there exists no coherent International Law regarding intervention. States disagree on the fundamental issues which require a consensus for rules to work. He points out that the case by case nature of decisions (or non-decisions) to intervene leave too much room for abuse. (50) No legal remedy exists, such as a Charter amendment, because of a lack of international consensus. Therefore, we are witnessing the emergence of coalitions which weigh the costs versus the benefits of intervention.

Just Wars Doctrine

There is a concept often referred to as the *Just Wars Doctrine*. The tenets of the doctrine include the principles that war is a last resort, it is directly waged to redress a wrong, it re-establishes peace, it is proportional, it does more good than harm and it is waged under legitimate authority. (51) The Just Wars Doctrine is not a principle of International Law in part because states tend to believe that each of the belligerents may have a "just cause." However, it does take on the color of common law because its tenets are often used as a reference or justification for the use of force. In any case, the doctrine could be the basis for some rules regarding the use of force.

Responsibility to Protect

The *Responsibility to Protect* it is a relatively new concept. From 2001 through 2005 it evolved from an idea to a concept endorsed by the United Nations. It has been part of international debates regarding the protection of populations from mass atrocities. It has been referred to in numerous resolutions by both the United Nations Security Council and the General Assembly. (52) The debates focus on whether or not the international community has an "obligation to intervene" or that it "should intervene" and to what extent. It was clearly endorsed by the United Nations General Assembly's 2005 World Summit Agreement even though the Responsibility to Protect is only the subject of three paragraphs in the Summit's forty page document. (53) The trend seems to be in the direction of "obligation" in International Law.

Interestingly, Article 1 of the Convention on the Prevention and Punishment of the Crime of Genocide adopted in 1948 was rather succinct. While not calling it the Responsibility to Protect, Article 1 states: "The contracting parties confirm that genocide, whether committed in time of peace or in time of war, is a crime under International Law which they undertake to prevent and punish." Still, as with many international issues, states tend to make their own interpretation.

What are the components of the Responsibility to Protect, and what events would trigger International intervention? The Responsibility to Protect has two propositions: First and foremost, it is the obligation of the "host" state to resolve the problem. If they are unable or unwilling, only then would outside states intervene. The triggering component includes four mass atrocity crimes: (1) genocide; (2) war crimes; (3) ethnic cleansing, and (4) crimes against humanity. (54) This component is founded in International Law. The second proposition of the Responsibility to Protect states that the International community not only has the right but the collective responsibility to assist the host state and to act when the host state is unable or unwilling to protect their population. The Responsibility to Protect posits that intervention is not just a discretionary right but a positive duty of the International community. (55) It must be pointed out that this proposition is not (yet) International Law. Dr. Simon Adams, in his essay, "Libya and the Responsibility to Protect" asserts that the responsibility of the International community is to "act, not necessarily to intervene." (56)

The Responsibility to Protect is usually considered to be categorically distinct from most definitions of humanitarian intervention. Responsibility to Protect seeks to establish a clearer code of conduct for humanitarian interventions and also advocates a greater reliance on non-military measures. This responsibility is said to involve three stages: to prevent, to react, and to rebuild. (57)

Humanitarian Intervention

Dr. Adams states that the Responsibility to Protect is designed to prevent atrocities and that it differs from *Humanitarian Intervention*. He tells us that Humanitarian Intervention is far broader than the Responsibility to Protect in that it focuses on military intervention by the International community upon a state committing the crimes without that state's consent to intervene. (58) Marco Marjanovic claims that, "Humanitarian Intervention has been defined as a state's use of "military force (publicly stated that its use is for ending the violation of human rights) against another state." (59) However, might Humanitarian Intervention also include non-military forms of intervention such as *Humanitarian aid* and *International sanctions*? David Scheffer states that, "Humanitarian Intervention should be understood to encompass… non-forcible methods, namely intervention undertaken without military force to alleviate mass human suffering within sovereign borders." (60)

Humanitarian Intervention may allow the use of force in a situation where the United Nations Security Council cannot pass a resolution under Chapter VII of the Charter of the United Nations due to veto by a permanent member.

There is a general consensus on some of its essential characteristics: (61)

1. Humanitarian intervention involves the threat and use of military forces as a central feature.

2. It is an intervention in the sense that it entails interfering in the internal affairs of a state by sending military forces into the territory or airspace of a sovereign state that has not committed an act of aggression against another state.

3. The intervention is in response to situations that do not necessarily pose direct threats to states' strategic interests, but instead is motivated by humanitarian objectives.

To its proponents, Humanitarian Intervention advocates action in the face of human rights abuses, over the rights of state sovereignty. To its detractors it is often viewed as a pretext for military intervention, often without legal sanction and possibly used to achieve the results desired by the intervening state.

Dr. Adams states that the Responsibility to Protect is designed to prevent atrocities and that it differs from *Humanitarian Intervention*. He tells us that Humanitarian Intervention is far broader than the Responsibility to Protect in that it focuses on military intervention by the International community upon a state committing humanitarian crimes without that offending state's consent to intervene. (62)

Right of Self-defense

Under what circumstances does a state have the *Right of Self-defense*? The United Nations Charter clearly states in Article 51: "Nothing in the present Charter shall impair the inherent right of individual or collective self-defence (sic) if an armed attack occurs against a Member of the United Nations, until the Security Council has taken necessary measures to maintain international peace and security". We must keep in mind that the Charter was written when international conflict primarily consisted of "tanks amassing on the border". International Law is woefully deficient in dealing with today's non-state actor attacks. As a result it has been alleged that Article 51 may be the most abused article in the Charter. States will invoke Article 51 even when they only "feel" threatened.

Scholars differ as to the interpretation of Article 51. Mary Ellen O'Connell in her article, "Self-Defense" quotes several scholars: (63) Derek Bowett argues against the need for an actual armed conflict to occur, stressing that the "inherent" Right of Self-defense refers to customary International Law as restated in the 1841 correspondence over the sinking of the *Caroline*. The S.S. Caroline was a United States vessel carrying arms and supplies for Canadian rebels. When it crossed into Canadian waters, Canadian and British forces captured the ship, released the crew, set the Caroline on fire and sent it over Niagara Falls. While there was no aggressive action on the part of the Caroline's crew, the Canadians and the British justified their action as the Right of Self-defense.

Derek Bowett urges that, in the absence of "any centralized machinery for the enforcement of the law," the need for greater self-help is "obvious". (64) Stanimir Alexandrov returns to Bowett's arguments that force in self-defense may be exercised in more situations than armed attack and that this reading is justified by the Security Council's failure to take effective action to ensure international peace and security. (65) Ian Brownlie provides a point-by-point response to Bowett, including a history of Articles 2(4) and 51 to demonstrate that only a strict interpretation of the Charter rules is reasonable. (66)

In 2005 the United Nations completed a two-year review of the Charter and United Nations operations. The final document, "World Summit Outcome 2005", recommitted the members to strict adherence to Charter terms. The document adds no additional support for a right to attack in self-defense in situations other than an armed attack. (67) This position appears to be in direct conflict with the United Nations position on the Responsibility to Protect at this same World Summit Outcome 2005, which again illustrates the ambiguities in International Law.

Preemptive Strikes

Typically, the use of the term *Preemptive Strikes* is described as one state taking military action against another state which it fears is preparing an aggressive action. As we can see, by the characterization of self-defense described above, the two are linked. Additionally, the Just Wars Doctrine plays into the equation.

The issue of preemptive strikes is hotly debated. The United Nations Charter Article 2.4 states, "Members…shall refrain…from the threat or use of force against the territorial integrity or political independence of any state..". Article 42 states that "….the Security

Council…may take such actions by air, sea or land forces as may be necessary…". Taken together, they would imply that the Security Council is the sole authority on the use of force. There is an exception in the Charter with Article 51, "Nothing in the present Charter shall impair the inherent right of individual or collective self-defense….". Within Article 51 the phrase "…if an armed attack occurs…", would imply, according to some detractors to the use of Preemptive Strikes, a strict interpretation of Article 51 would indicate that states may only use force after an attack.

Nowhere in International Law are preemptive strikes considered legal. Therefore, states rely more heavily on an attempt at a broad interpretation of Article 51, the right of self-defense. Opponents of preemptive strikes argue that a liberal interpretation of Article 51 would leave wide room for abuse, in fact, the tactic points to the potential of aggressive abuse. Because of that potential abuse, these opponents argue that Preemptive Strikes should never be allowed.

International Law scholars, Michael Byers and Simon Chesterman, go to great lengths to argue against changing the rules in International Law to render unilateral intervention legal. (68)

Perhaps anticipating criticism, the National Security Strategy (NSS) explicitly contends that the preemptive option is firmly grounded in

International Law: "For centuries, International Law recognized that nations need not suffer an attack before they can lawfully take action to defend themselves against forces that present an imminent danger of attack". (69)

Some legal scholars and international jurists often conditioned the legitimacy of preemption on the existence of an imminent threat, most often a visible mobilization of armies, navies, and air forces preparing to attack. The position of these scholars and jurists is that, "We must adapt the concept of imminent threat to the capabilities and objectives of today's adversaries. Rogue states and terrorists do not seek to attack us using conventional means. They know such attacks would fail. Instead, they rely on acts of terror and, potentially, the use of weapons of mass destruction, weapons that can be easily concealed, delivered covertly, and used without warning. (70) In other words, the law of self-defense has long permitted military action in anticipation of an imminent attack. However, the requirement of imminency (sic) must evolve as the nature of the threat changes". After providing the legal justification for preemption, the NSS enunciates "the standard(s) by which….(a state)…will act. The greater the threat, the greater is the risk of inaction, and the more compelling the case for taking anticipatory action to defend…., even if uncertainty remains as to the time and place of the enemy's attack. Does this standard comport with International Law? ….. the answer(s) to such question(s) depend on the facts at hand in each individual case". (71)

Richard Shultz and Andreas Vogt, of the Fletcher School of Law and Diplomacy, put the matter of Preemptive Strikes most succinctly. They posit that morally, the inclusion of preemptive operations in the concept of self-defense (defensive intervention) is anchored in the Just Wars Doctrine. They also believe that the presumption in favor of self-defense is so strong that the Just Wars Doctrine does not confine itself exclusively to defensive measures and the legacy of the non-intervention rule. Shultz and Vogt argue that offensive operations are permitted to protect vital rights and interests unjustly threatened, not only injured by other states, but also by non-state actors such as terrorist groups. (72)

According to Antonio Cassese, "It would be naïve and self-defeating to contend that a state should wait for the attack by another country, in the full knowledge that it is certain to take place. It is argued that to impose on states the attitude of 'sitting ducks' when confronted with an impending military attack makes a mockery, both in its acceptability to states and of the Charter's main purpose of minimizing unauthorized coercion and violence across state lines". (73) Could it be assumed that Cassese's argument would include non-state actors?

SECTION THREE

THE JUSTIFICATIONS FOR OR AGAINST

MUSLIM VIOLENCE

Muslim armed conflicts with the West span from the eighth century up to the present day. Early on, the conquest and the reclaiming of "Holy" sites by both the Muslims and European Christendom also included the Crusades.

If one accepts the concept that the Muslim world is justified in their animosity toward the West, that they believe their religious, cultural and social values, and indeed, their territorial states are under siege or attack, they have the right of self-defense. That right is recognized in International Law and by the United Nations. Article 51 of the United Nations Charter, referring to an "armed attack", specifically justifies that right.

Article 51 further states that the besieged "Member" (of the United Nations) must immediately report such actions of self-defense to the Security Council and that it is the responsibility of the Security Council "…to take at any time such actions as it deems necessary in order to maintain or restore international peace and security". (74) The Muslim

world could argue that the Soviet Invasion during the 1980's was an act of

aggression. They would probably be right. However, in 1980 the United

Nations Security Council's resolution to condemn the Soviet Union was

vetoed by the Soviet Union.

The 1991 Gulf War, also known as Operation Desert Storm, was

led by the United States to reverse Saddam Hussein's invasion of Kuwait.

For the Muslim world to declare that the invasion of Iraq by the West was

an act of aggression ran into a significant problem: Operation Desert

Storm was sanctified by the United Nations.

The Muslim world could argue that the United States' led NATO

invasion of Afghanistan beginning on October 7, 2001, a month after the

September 11, 2001 attack on the World Trade Center and the NATO

invasion of Iraq in 2003 as just such acts of armed aggression. Their

chance of success with the Security Council would likely be fruitless

given that several members of the Security Council who hold the veto

power would be the target of the Muslim petition. Interestingly, the

United States could argue that the Afghan invasion was legal under Article

51, or the Just Wars Doctrine. Additionally, if the self-defense argument

failed, the United States and the NATO allies could have argued legality under the concepts of the Responsibility to Protect, Genocide, and/or Crimes Against Humanity. These three concepts could have their basis in the Sunnis attacks against Shiites, Shiites against Sunnis, and in the case of Iraq, government attacks against Shiites. It is a given that those arguments would encounter opposition.

There is a problem. Both International Law and the United Nations have characterized both armed aggression and self-defense as between the armed forces of adversarial states, the so called "tanks amassing on the border". Unfortunately, that is not the nature of today's conflicts. Today's conflicts are more often characterized by guerrilla warfare and terrorist tactics. Those tactics worked rather well for the Israelis against the British after World War II. The British were resisting the formation of the state of Israel. In 1948 the Israelis proclaimed the state of Israel. The state of Israel was quickly recognized by many of the states of the world.

The question is, "Is the use of the terrorist actions employed by various Muslim groups justified?" To better understand and evaluate that question, an understanding of terrorism and terrorist groups is necessary.

What is terrorism?

The word "terrorism" is almost self-evident. It is violence

designed to do just that, strike terror in the minds of the intended victims. Today's terrorist organizations do strike strategic targets such as government facilities and military assets. However, more often they strike "soft" targets. Those soft targets often include, but are not limited to, restaurants, bus and train stations, airports, shopping centers and any location where large groups of people assemble. They will strike where people least expect violence such as small towns, sporting events and movie theaters. Targeting commercial airline flights has no military value but they do cause fear and involve major logistical security measures which are expensive. Protecting against terror attacks becomes an intelligence nightmare involving large amounts of manpower on the part of governments, the militaries and law enforcement.

Modern Terrorist Organizations

The confrontation with which the West is faced from the Muslim world comes from three sources: *Fundamentalists*; *True Believers*; and what is often called the "*Opportunists*".

The Fundamentalists are comprised of some mullahs and other influential leaders. They believe that Islam, their culture and their whole way of life is under threat from the Western influence. The True Believers are the followers of the Fundamentalist. This group consists of well-educated middle-class individuals and some of the working-class. While some do, many are not concerned with the fate of Islam. What is at issue is how the True Believers and the Fundamentalists have elected to go about combating the problem. For them the only thing sacred is the true belief in Allah and the Koran. For many of them anything that will create the ultimate triumph of Islam and a worldwide Caliph (Caliphate) under Sharia Law is justified in their minds.

They have found terrorism to be their most effective weapon. Islamic states, such as Iran, would fail miserably in an attempt to fight the West with conventional "state to state" combat. Western military prowess was graphically illustrated with the removal of Iraqi forces from Kuwait in 1991.

Additionally, to create strict adherence to the tenets of Islam, they justify violence, and in the Western view, intolerable injustice even to their own people. The West finds this oxymoronic. In their pursuit of pure Islam the Muslim world must come to grips with the fact that the Koran preaches tolerance, and there is a prohibition against killing, especially fellow Muslims.

The Opportunists are the hijackers of Islam. They use the Koran and the faith to justify their violent actions and their quest for power and control. In the case of the criminal Opportunists, their quest is purely financial gain. It is possible that there are many mullahs within this group whose true interest is to promote their power base. However, the majority of Opportunists are just plain criminals.

The average Muslim is not a major actor other than providing recruits for the Fundamentalist, True Believers and the Opportunists. They may become active participants if they accept the agenda of the Fundamentalist and the True Believers, or the propaganda of the Opportunists, or they perceive a Western injustice. If they perceive Western injustice, they may become sympathizers aiding the terrorist groups with financial support, shelter, and passive resistance to the Western attempts to combat the threat. Additionally, by not voicing outrage at the terrorist acts, the average Muslim appears to provide tacit approval to those acts.

One cannot omit government involvement. There are governments in the Islamic world who clandestinely support terrorist action. In some cases it may be out of true belief. However, it is possible that support may be for political gain.

There are three types of terrorist networks: *Lone Wolves*; *Cells*; and *Commanders and Cadres*. They each have their own set of challenges when it comes to effectively committing their acts of terrorism. (75)

The Lone Wolves are individuals, acting alone and controlled by no one. Generally, their motives are known only to themselves. In the United States the Unabomber was an exception: Theodore Kaczynski left notes and correspondence with the media. He started his bombing in 1978 and through 1994 he exploded sixteen bombs, killing three people and injuring twenty-three.

Because they are acting alone and controlled by no one, Lone Wolves are extremely difficult to apprehend. Even though many individuals may be on law enforcement's "radar", law enforcement may not know of the existence of some Lone Wolves until after they have attacked. However, their ability to do damage is considerably less than the other two groups. Timothy McVey and his bombing of the Alfred Murrah Federal Office Building in Oklahoma City on April 19, 1995 is the exception in that massive damage was done.

Cells are exactly what the name implies. They are individual groups tied by a common cause. However, their connection to one another is generally known only by very few members of each cell. Through that connection they are able to coordinate violence. They are capable of doing considerable damage. However, that capability may be hampered by breaks in communications, among other logistical problems. Because of their clandestine nature and their loose organization they are difficult to apprehend, but they can be penetrated.

Commanders and Cadres are nearly corporate in structure. Because of the hierarchy of command these terrorist organizations are able to coordinate violence much more effectively than the other two types. For this reason, Commanders and Cadres are capable of doing the most damage. However, because of their highly organized structure, Commanders and Cadres are the easiest to combat.

The 9/11/2001 destruction of the World Trade Center in New York using commercial airliners, the crashing of an airliner into the Pentagon in Washington D. C. and the downing of yet another commercial airliner in a field in Pennsylvania, all on the same day, was the work of al Qaeda as a Commanders and Cadres operation. Terrorist attacks such as the Madrid and London train bombings may have been executed by al Qaeda affiliated Cells. Since the 9/11 attack, the West's military and intelligence operation against al Qaeda is believed to have vastly disrupted al Qaeda's communications ability, and many of their leaders have been killed or captured. However, it should be noted that in recent years both al Qaeda and the Taliban have been making a resurgence.

Commanders and Cadres have the greatest capability to obtain financing, followed by Cells, with Lone Wolves having little opportunity for outside aid. From where does financing come? Some of the aid, both financial and materiel, comes from sympathetic governments. For example, the United States aided Afghan war lords in their fight against the Soviet Union. Iran and Syria are particularly suspected of aiding the various terrorist groups in the Middle East. Much of the aid comes from the *Diaspora*, the disbursed foreign Muslim community. The diaspora often utilizes what is known as *Hawala* which is the transfer of generally small sums of money with a handshake through Muslim brokers all over the world. Thus, they leave no paper trail.

Finally, there are the criminal sources. The Opportunists are mainly criminals and are in the fray primarily for personal gain. For some, terrorism has paid off handsomely. They engage in bank robbery, kidnapping for ransom, extortion, illegal arms trading, money laundering, prostitution, and trafficking in human slavery. Drug trafficking, primarily Afghan heroin, is a huge source of terrorist funding. (76) All of this illegal activity and the profits gained explain why, when an equitable solution to a conflict is at hand, one or more of the groups involved will find a way to torpedo the deal.

There are two terms that are important with respect to terrorist organizations ultimate goals. Those terms are the *"Near Enemy"* and the *"Far Enemy"*.

The Near Enemy refers to a localized enemy. The Taliban is a good example. Their primary objective is the removal of the West from Afghanistan and the Taliban control of the Afghan government.

al Qaeda and ISIS are examples of the goal of combating the Far Enemy. Their ambitions exceed any individual state's borders. They look to the eventual Islamic domination worldwide. Originally ISIS was confining their fight for conquest in Iraq and Syria. That goal has since been expanded to global conquest under Sharia law. They envision an ultimate cataclysmic final battle between "good and evil".

To analyze whether or not the tactics being employed by the various Muslim groups are justified or even "legal" under International Law, we can look to the Geneva Conventions (77) for guidance. The Geneva Conventions are a series of international agreements primarily for

Establishing the *Rules of War*. They were drafted between 1864 and 1949. Two additional protocols to the 1949 agreement were added in 1977. Most "civilized" states and most people have standards of human value and dignity. Therefore, most of the states of the world recognize and adhere to the Geneva Conventions' rules for the conduct of armed conflict. While International Law functions only so long as states agree to follow the edicts thereof, the Geneva Conventions have been a major influence on the definitions of what constitutes, for example, Crimes Against Humanity and Genocide. The International Criminal Court has had successful prosecutions in recent years. One could argue that the Nazi hierarchy received a dubious fair trail, nonetheless the Nuremberg Trials were guided in part by the Geneva Conventions.

It must be understood that the Geneva Conventions do not recognize terrorism as a legitimate tactic of conflict, in fact, quite the contrary. Convention III of August 12, 1949 Section I, paragraph a). defines the requirements for an armed force of a party to be recognized as a legitimate force. The combatants must be organized and placed under a command responsible to that party for the conduct of its subordinates. Under Article 4 of the Third Convention the armed force does not necessarily need to be represented by a government so long as they comply with the Conventions. Other than the occasional news or intelligence report, it is unknown to what degree organizations (*parties*) such as ISIS, al Qaeda or the Taliban subscribe to this provision. Additionally, armed forces must be subject to an internal disciplinary system which complies with International Law. It would be difficult for Muslim terrorist organizations to argue that they are in compliance with that provision. Paragraph a.) of Section One of the 1949 agreement requires that the combatants be distinguished by a recognizable uniform or other distinctive sign. ISIS could argue that the display of their flag constitutes compliance. If the combatants do not have a uniform or other recognizable means of identification, they must have their weapons in plain sight. Suicide belts or vests do not comply. Violations of these provisions could deprive a captured combatant of certain protections afforded by the Conventions' requirements for the treatment of prisoners of war.

The Conventions clearly state that captured combatants and captured civilians are entitled to respect for their lives, dignity, personal rights and convictions. They shall be protected against all acts of violence. Is the wholesale killing by execution of civilians, the beheading of both civilians and combatants and in some cases, the burning alive of some captives, gross violations of these provisions? There are constant news reports of these types of violations, and often, the terrorist organizations brag about or display such killings.

The Conventions state that adversaries must distinguish between civilian populations and combatants in order to spare civilian populations and property. Civilian populations cannot be the object of attack. The news media occasionally report that the Muslim organizations place civilians around military targets and use mosques as forts or arms storage facilities in the belief that Western forces will not attack those facilities.

Apparently the Western militaries believe this is the case which creates a tactical dilemma.

The Conventions state that the purposeful killing and capturing of civilian groups because of their ethnicity or religion could be characterized as Genocide or Crimes Against Humanity. Is the deliberate killing of Christians by ISIS an example?

The Conventions also state that attacks shall be directed solely against military objects. Therefore, are not the bombings and firearms attacks against civilian restaurants, bus, train stations and commercial airports and aircraft clear violations? The deliberate destruction of religious sites, historical sites, archeological sites and works of art do not qualify as legitimate tactics of armed conflict.

Many of the tactics here described are employed by the various Muslim organizations. The Geneva Conventions, in the sections discussing sanctions, classify some of these tactics as "gross violations" which could be interpreted as "War Crimes" and punishable by an international tribunal.

If, in fact, these tactics are not justified, what are the Muslims to do with respect to their fears of Western domination? The Internet effectively prevents insulation from Western influence. Could diplomacy create a situation where the West would agree to withdraw, in whole or in part, both militarily and commercially, from Islamic lands? If, in fact, the Muslims would agree to negotiate, it is reasonable to assume that the Muslims believe that negotiations would be futile.

Could recognized state governments effectively expel western states from their land? With the possible exception of Iran, very little has been tried with this tactic. Iran's attempts have resulted in an increase of the animosities. State involvement has almost always been necessary to achieve a positive result in major international disputes.

THE WEST'S JUSTIFICATION FOR OR AGAINST ITS
CURRENT ACTIONS

As a point of clarification, the use of the term "the West" means the coalition of members of the North Atlantic Treaty Organization (NATO) as well as other non-member European states. The United States is the lead member state in the conflicts with Muslim terrorists. The militaries of some Middle Eastern states are included. States such as Iraq and Saudi Arabia have contributing forces. Turkey and other Gulf states have contributed support. For the most part, Israel's participation focuses mainly on the Palestinians, Hezbollah and Hamas. Western states have declared that Hezbollah and Hamas are terrorist organizations.

The same criteria used to analyze the Muslim world's reaction to their grievances will be used to analyze the West's reaction to the Muslim tactics. That is, the United Nations Charter, the Geneva Conventions and the *customary* interpretation of International Law will be employed. That presents yet another dilemma. As referred to in the last section, both the United Nations Charter and the Geneva Conventions were written at the time when international conflicts mainly consisted of "tanks amassing on the border". That is, conflict was typically states against states employing uniformed militaries. That is not the situation today.

On one side, even though organized and coordinated in some cases, the Muslim combatants are quite often indistinguishable from the general population. With the West, combatants are usually uniformed in organized and disciplined armed forces. Therefore, in the experiences of the West, the Muslims are waging "Unconventional Warfare". This condition creates highly subjective political policy and military decisions for all the combatants. This is not meant to excuse the possibility of violations of International Law by the West. Rather, it is meant to emphasize the difficulty in trying to analyze the West's actions.

It is interesting to note that the West's (primarily the United States) clandestine support of the Afghan Muslim warlords in their successful expulsion of the Soviet troops in the 1980's should have created a bond between the West and the Muslim world. It did not. In fact, some Muslim terrorist groups conducted attacks on Western interests. The attacks occurred both before and after the West's military actions in Afghanistan and Iraq.

The following is just a sampling of those attacks. 1). There were two attacks in Lebanon. On April 18, 1983 the United States embassy was attacked, killing 63 people. Then again on October 23, 1983 the United

States Marine barracks in a Beirut attack resulted in 243 United States Marines dead along with 58 French soldiers. 2). Pan Am flight 103 was bombed over Lockerbie, Scotland on December 21, 1988 killing all 243 passengers and the flight crew of 16. 3). The U.S.S. Cole was attacked on October 12, 2000 which killed 17 United States Navy sailors and injured 37 others. 4). September 11, 2001 saw the al Qaeda attack on the World Trade Center and the Pentagon. Between the aircraft deaths, the Towers deaths and the Pentagon deaths, 2,996 people died and a further estimated 6,000 were injured. 5). The Cercanias Commuter Rail System in the Atocha Train Station in Madrid, Spain on April 11, 2004 was bombed. That attack was coordinated with a total of 10 bombs on 4 trains in 3 stations. 191 people died and an estimated 2000 were injured.

Given the clandestine nature of these attacks, would one or more of the International Law principles discussed above justify retaliation, even across state lines, assuming the attackers could be identified?

Iraq: 1991-1992

This analysis will begin with U. S. President George H. W. Bush creating a coalition of states to forcibly remove Saddam Hussein's Iraqi troops from Kuwait in 1991/1992. In that case, Hussein was given ample opportunity by both the United Nations and the United States to withdraw.

He chose not to do so, and the Western military intervention expelled Iraqi troops from Kuwait. Was that action justified or legal? Could the argument for the *Responsibility to Protect* be invoked in the Kuwaiti intervention? Or, could it be argued that the intervention was solely to protect Western oil interests? If so, would that military intervention be characterized instead as illegal aggression?

In its entire history, with some 170 plus significant violent conflicts, the United Nations has only been proactive twice. The first was the intervention in the Korean conflict in the early 1950's. That action was only possible because the Soviet Union walked out of the Security Council deliberations and therefore failed to exercise its veto. The expelling of Iraq from Kuwait was the second. Even then, the United Nations did not contribute a military force. Rather, it condoned the actions of the Western powers. There was a lack of worldwide protest. However, there has been constant argument as to whether or not that intervention was legal or illegal under International Law.

The conflicts in Afghanistan and the 2003 invasion of Iraq must be treated separately. The dynamics of each of them is different. We will begin with Afghanistan in the aftermath of 9/11. The reader is reminded to refer to the descriptions of (1) *Genocide*, (2) *Crimes Against Humanity*,

(3) *Aggression,* (4) *Sovereignty,* (5) *Responsibilities of Sovereignty,* (6) the *Piercing of Sovereignty,* (7) *Intervention,* (8) the *Just Wars Doctrine,* (9) *Responsibility to Protect,* (10) *Right of Self-defense* and (11) *Preemptive Strikes* to help make a judgment as to whether or not the West's actions were justified.

Afghanistan: 2001-2002

Osama bin Laden was a well-educated and well-traveled leader. He understood world politics (78) and by all accounts his apparent goal was a worldwide jihad. In August 1998 the United States attacked al Qaeda's training camps in Afghanistan in retaliation for al Qaeda's attacks on the United States embassies in Tanzania and Kenya. (79) Could that retaliatory attack be justified as an act of self-defense? International Law recognizes that a state's embassy in a foreign state technically is the territory of that embassy's state.

That said, the exception in the United Nations Charter to the prohibition of the use of force is found in Article 51 of the Charter, the Right of Self-defense. Article 51 of the Charter states in part: "Nothing in the present Charter shall impair the inherent right of individual or collective self-defence (sic) if an armed attack occurs against a Member of the United Nations..." Article 51 goes on to require the attacked state to report to the Security Council and, if they deem necessary, the Security Council to take measures to restore peace. (80)

With the September 11, 2001 al Qaeda attack on the World Trade Center in New York and the Pentagon in Washington, D.C., the United States initiated a full scale offensive against al Qaeda in their Afghanistan stronghold. al Qaeda retreated to the Mountains of Tora Bora along the border with Pakistan. Is it reasonable to assume that the United States was invoking its right to self-defense? If the World Trade Center and the Pentagon attacks had been the work of a recognized state employing missiles, there would have probably been no question as to the right of the United States to retaliate.

Apparently much of the world agreed, and the United States was successful in bringing the North Atlantic Treaty Organization (NATO) into the subsequent actions in Afghanistan. Even Pakistan cooperated initially with the United States' bombing of al Qaeda in Tora Bora by stationing its troops on the border with Tora Bora. (81) NATO invoked Article 5 of the NATO Charter, "An attack on one is an attack on all".(82) However, NATO made no military commitment at that time.

The United Nations passed a resolution urging "…all nations to redouble their efforts…" to combat terrorism. With a second resolution the United Nations declared that all nations should "…suppress the financing of terrorism…" (83) While the United Nations did not give the United States a free hand, 30 states pledged military support. (84)

Subsequently, in December, 2001, the United Nations Security Council established the International Security Assistance Force (ISAF) to oversee military operations. (85) In 2003 NATO took command of the International Security Assistance Force. (86) The United States participated under that umbrella but the United States did maintain forces under its sole command. (87)

The Taliban effectively controlled Afghanistan. With the logic that the Taliban harbored al Qaeda and failed to acquiesce to ultimatums by the United States to hand over bin Laden and his followers, the United States, NATO, the ISAF and Afghan government forces proceeded to expel the Taliban from Afghanistan.

The Afghan "war" continues. In 2003, with the shift in focus to Iraq by the West, the Taliban and al Qaeda began a resurgence and continued attacks on United States, NATO, ISAF and Afghan government forces. The West justifies its continuing fight as an attempt to rebuild Afghanistan, with a stable government and a continued fight against terrorism. (Note: The United States began a drawdown of its military forces beginning in 2011. As of 2016, approximately 8,600 United States troops remain.)

Is the continued NATO, ISAF and the Afghan government's fight legal under International Law? Critics say no. al Qaeda is not a state and, under the requirements of Article 51 of the United Nations Charter, they assert that no follow up "imminent attack" was coming from al Qaeda. Defenders of the action advocate that the current actions, given al Qaeda and Taliban actions and threats, are acts of self-defense and clearly allowed under Article 51. The West could possibly advocate that the operations could be legal under Humanitarian Intervention. The debate continues. One thing is clear to this author, the United Nations, and therefore, International Law has not adequately addressed terrorist warfare.

Iraq: 2003-Present

Was the United States invasion of Iraq and the removal and subsequent capture of Iraqi president Saddam Hussein legal under International Law? The ostensible reason for the invasion was the belief that Hussein possessed weapons of mass destruction (WMD). While there was ample evidence that he once had them, (witness the gassing of the Kurds in the north and the Shiites in the south) none were found. If the belief in the existence of weapons of mass destruction was genuine, what led to that conviction? A little background in the run-up to the invasion is in order.

Following the end of the Gulf War in 1991, United Nations Security Council Resolution 687 directed the International Atomic Energy Agency (IAEA) to find and dismantle Iraq's nuclear weapons program, and ensure Iraqi compliance with the Nuclear Non-Proliferation Treaty through comprehensive ongoing monitoring and verification. Resolution 687 was adopted following the Persian Gulf War. It called for Iraq to destroy all of its chemical, biological weapons and missiles with a range of greater than 150 kilometers. Resolution 687 also prohibited Iraq from developing nuclear weapons and to submit a declaration of its weapons program. Finally, the resolution called for voluntary on-site inspections.

Despite this broad and unprecedented mandate, the IAEA initially received only minimal cooperation from Iraq. In its first declaration to the IAEA, Iraq failed to disclose the existence of electromagnetic isotope separators (EMIS) uranium enrichment facilities at Al-Tarmiya and Ash Sharqat, as well as its weaponization research. Nevertheless, inspections revealed much of the program and forced Iraq to admit to its weapons aspirations, including research at Tuwaitha and Al-Atheer. [88][89]

Between May 1991 and October 1997 the IAEA completed a series of 30 inspection campaigns, oversaw the destruction and disablement of nuclear facilities, and removed all weapons-usable nuclear material from Iraq. (90)(91) Through late 1998 the IAEA continued to monitor Iraq's nuclear activities despite the regime's reluctance to cooperate fully.

Following Saddam's announcement in October 1998 that he would end all cooperation with United Nations inspectors, the United Nations Special Commission (UNSCOM) Chairman Richard Butler issued a scathing report to the Security Council detailing Iraq's efforts to obstruct the Commission's mandate. (92)(93) The report became the basis for the December 1998 U.S. and British bombing campaign known as Operation Desert Fox. (94)(95) IAEA and United Nations inspectors withdrew from Iraq that same month, and Saddam did not permit their reentry for another four years.

In January 2001, a United States Defense Department report assessed that "Iraq would need five or more years and key foreign assistance to rebuild the infrastructure to enrich enough material for a nuclear weapon." The Defense Department added that the amount of time needed (96)(97) could be "substantially shortened" if Iraq obtained fissile material from a foreign source. Facing the prospect of a United

States invasion and claims that it had weapons of mass destruction, Iraq permitted IAEA inspectors to resume verification activities within the country.

Prior to 2002, the United Nations Security Council had passed 16 resolutions on Iraq. In 2002, the Security Council unanimously passed Resolution 1441. With Resolution 1441 Iraq was given "a final opportunity" to comply with its nuclear, biological an chemical disarmament obligations. The United States' position was that Iraq was not cooperating with United Nations inspectors and had not met its obligations to 17 United Nations Security Council resolutions. The United States felt that Resolution 1441 called for the immediate, total unilateral disarmament of Iraq. The United States continued to show frustration at the fact that months after the resolution was passed Iraq was still not disarming. Resolution 1441 recalled that the use of "all means necessary" was still authorized and in effect from Resolution 678. Therefore, the United States maintained that if Iraq failed to comply with the "one final chance to comply" with the provisions of Resolution 1441, then military action would be the result. (98)

In early December 2002, Iraq filed a 12,000-page weapons declaration with the United Nations. After reviewing the document, United Nations weapons inspectors, the United States, France, United

Kingdom and other countries thought that this declaration failed to account for all of Iraq's chemical and biological agents. Interestingly, many of these countries had supplied the Iraqi regime with the technology to make these weapons in the 1980s during the Iran–Iraq War.

On December 19, 2002 United States Secretary of State Colin Powell stated that Iraq was in "material breach" of the Security Council resolution. (99) Great Britain was the greatest supporter of the United States' position. On January 20, 2003, French Foreign Minister Dominique de Villepin said, "We think that military intervention would be the worst possible solution." However, France believed that Iraq may have maintained an ongoing chemical and nuclear weapons program. (100)

On February 5, 2003, Powell appeared before the United Nations to prove the urgency to engage in a war with Iraq. Although the presentation failed to change the fundamental position of the Security Council, including France, Russia, China, and Germany, Powell succeeded in hardening the overall tone of the United Nations toward Iraq. (101)

On the same day, Russian Foreign Minister Igor Ivanov said that Russia's position was that there was no evidence justifying war with Iraq. However, Russia's opinion shifted following a report by the United Nations inspectors stating that while Iraq cooperated on a "practical" level, they had not demonstrated "genuine acceptance" to disarm.

Vladimir Putin stated that, if things did not change and Iraq continued to defy complete cooperation with inspectors, Russia would support a United States led invasion. Putin conditioned that statement on the United States not going it alone and working through the United Nations Security Council. (102)

Iraq had retained its nuclear expertise, including design information, scientists and engineers, and a powerful and effective concealment apparatus. However, IAEA Director General Mohamed El-Baradei reported to the Security Council on March 7, 2003 that, "After three months of intrusive inspections, we have to date found no evidence or plausible indications of the revival of a nuclear weapons program in Iraq." (103)(104)

After the March 7, 2003 United Nations Monitoring, Verification and Inspection Commission's Hans Blix Report, the United States and the other members of the "Coalition of the Willing" reaffirmed their belief that Iraq was still in material breach of Resolution 687. (105) The United States lobbied for a new resolution which would authorize an invasion of Iraq. It was aborted when it became apparent that United Nations Security Council resistance was just too great. Nevertheless, on March 20, 2003 the "Coalition of the Willing" invaded Iraq principally for the removal Saddam Hussain, and the Coalition believed, eliminate Iraq's weapons of mass destruction. Saddam was removed from power in April 2003. Subsequently, with Resolution 1483, the United Nations declared that the United States and the United Kingdom were "occupying powers" under International Law with legitimate authority over Iraq. The United Nations then lifted the economic sanctions imposed on Iraq during the 1991 Gulf War.

After the Second Gulf War the United States Central Intelligence Agency's Iraq Survey Group (ISG) was tasked with uncovering evidence of Iraq's alleged illicit WMD programs. In its comprehensive report issued on September 30, 2004, the ISG concluded there was no evidence to suggest that a coordinated effort to restart Iraq's nuclear program had existed since the first Gulf War ended in 1991. (106)(107)

However, inspectors found that Saddam Hussein had planned to recreate his weapons of mass destruction (WMD) programs after the lifting of international sanctions. The ISG report states that as early as 1991, Saddam told his advisors he wanted to continue to employ Iraq's nuclear scientists, a theme the report claims "persisted throughout the sanctions period." (108)(109) Since Iraq lacked the ability to continue the program at its full potential, Saddam instead sought to deter adversaries by falsely aggrandizing Iraq's overall WMD capabilities. (110)(111) Even so, on September 16, 2004, United Nations General Secretary Kofi Annan stated that the invasion was "not in conformity with the United Nations Charter" and was therefore illegal under International Law. (112)

As a result of the ISG's findings, the United States Congress arranged for a Senate Committee inquiry into the U.S. intelligence community's prewar assessments on Iraq. In a formal report released in March 2005, the committee accused the intelligence community of using insufficient sources, being too wedded to previous assumptions, and failing to conduct substantial research on the issues. The report states the intelligence community was "almost completely wrong" in its assumptions about Iraq's nuclear program. (113)(114) Most intelligence agencies faced accusations about their failures prior to the invasion, including the National Security, Central Intelligence, Defense Intelligence, and National Geospatial-Intelligence Agencies.

Powell himself stated later, "I, of course regret the U. N. speech that I gave," he said, "which became the prominent presentation of our case. But we thought it was correct at the time. The President thought it was correct. Congress thought it was correct. Of course I regret that a lot of it turned out be wrong." (115)

Given all of this, it would be easy to declare that the actions of the United States, Great Britain and "Coalition of the Willing" were clearly illegal under International Law as Kofi Annan so declared. However, is there a counter argument? Given Saddam's well documented actions and behaviors, if the United States, et. al. truly considered Iraq an imminent and serious threat, under International Law the invasion could have been characterized as a Preemptive Strike. Most scholars of International Law contend that Preemptive Strikes are never legal. In Section Three we saw that perhaps anticipating criticism, the National Security Strategy (NSS) explicitly contends that the preemptive option is firmly grounded in International Law: For centuries, International Law recognized that nations need not suffer an attack before they can lawfully take action to defend themselves against forces that present an imminent danger of attack.

Also Section Three pointed out that the Just Wars Doctrine does not confine itself exclusively to defensive measures and the legacy of the non-intervention rule. Shultz and Vogt argue that, "Offensive operations are permitted to protect vital rights and interests unjustly threatened, not only injured by other states, but also by non-state actors such as terrorist groups". Consider again the writings of Antonio Cassese, "It would be naïve and self-defeating to contend that a state should wait for the attack by another country, in the full knowledge that it is certain to take place. It is argued that to impose on states the attitude of 'sitting ducks' when confronted with an impending military attack makes a mockery, both in its acceptability to states and of the Charter's main purpose of minimizing unauthorized coercion and violence across state lines".

The aftermath of the removal of Saddam Hussein created chaos. The Iraqi military was disbanded. That created unemployment for any number of Iraqi young men and Iraqi military officers. Many of them, with resentment, joined budding forces with the intent to drive the Western forces out and to reinstate the old sectarian fighting between Sunni and Shiite populations.

While Saddam's repressive government was ostensibly secular, it was primarily dominated by the Sunni minority. With the removal of Hussein, the Coalition backed government was dominated by Shiites. The acts of terrorism by both Sunnis and Shiites against each other ensued and continues to this day.

Is it possible that justification of the Western actions could be found in International Law's Humanitarian Intervention and in the Responsibility to Protect? al Qaeda's and the Taliban's treatment of the people of Afghanistan, Saddam's treatment of the Iraqi people, the terrorist warfare between Sunnis and Shiites killing innocent people, and since 2014, the Islamic State's (ISIS) mass killings, beheadings and other atrocities comes quickly to mind. We must keep in mind that the

Responsibility to Protect is not yet International Law even though it is widely recognized. It is the reader's responsibility to decide if any of these arguments are valid.

THE ONGOING QUESTIONS

When one looks at the violent events going on in today's world, it is most difficult to remain objective. Depending on which side of the conflicts one has sympathy, it is easy to proclaim the moral and legal high ground on one's side and the criminal actions of the opposing side.

This paper has made no attempt to solve the problems associated with today's conflicts. Rather, it is hoped that the reader will employ their own powers of critical thinking to the issues raised. As a final note, a summary of some of the major questions is in order.

Possibly, the first question that needs to be asked is, "who started this?" It is somewhat like the schoolyard fight being broken up by a teacher with each combatant claiming the other is to blame. This paper has brought attention to the fact that neither the Muslim world nor the West is blameless. There is guilt on both sides.

Given that a vast majority of the casualties are Muslims against Muslims, should the conflicts be viewed as an intra-religious fight in which the West should not intervene? Or, as suggested above, does the international community have a duty to intervene?

Is there any way mass killings, suicide bombings, beheadings and the targeting of "soft targets" justified? By the same standards, are drone strikes aimed at specific targets but which kill innocent bystanders justified?

Even though torture is condemned by International Law and the Geneva Conventions, is some degree of torture, waterboarding for example, justified to extract valuable information? Critics say no, the victim will only tell their adversary what they believe the adversary wants to hear. On the other hand, the West claims that valuable intelligence has been obtained thereby.

Are the terrorist acts such as shootings and bombings outside the theaters of conflict legitimate offensive or defensive actions? Given those acts, are the continued aggressive actions by the West legitimate offensive or defensive actions?

Would, as some argue, the conflicts stop if the West withdrew its military and economic penetration of the Muslim world? Or, as some elements within the Muslim world have declared, they will fight the West to the death?

Finally, is Islam truly in danger from the West? Or, for that matter, is the West truly in danger from Islam?

REFERENCES

1. MacRae, Peter, Essay, "Do We Have Cause To Fear Islam?", San Diego, CA., 5/2005

2. Internet, Original Birth-name of Prophet Muhammud (pbuh), www.aaiil.org

3. Lewis, Bernard, *What Went Wrong*, Oxford, Oxford University Press, 2002

4. Kamen, Henry, *Spain 1469-1714. A Society in Conflict,* 3rd Edition, 37-38, Routledge Taylor and Francis Group, London/New York, 2005

5. Internet, "Crusades: facts and Summary", www.history.com/topics/crusades

6. Ibid

7. Ibid

8. Internet, "The Dark History of the Knights Templar", www.bibliotedapleyades.net/sociopolitical/Templars/knights/templar01.htm

9. Stewart. Desmond, *The Monks of War*, England, Penguin, 2000

10. Internet, "The Dark History of the Knights Templar", www.bibliotedapleyades.net/sociopolitical/Templars/knights/templar01.htm

11. Internet, Madden, Thomas, "The Real History of the Crusades", http://www.catholicity.com/commentary/madden/03463.html

12. Internet, "The Atlantic Slave Trade" History of Islam Encyclopedia, http://historyofislam.com/contents/onset-of-the-colonial-age/the-atlantic-slave-trade/

13. Ibid

14. Internet, "The Impact of the European Colonization of the Middle East on Modern Arab Societies", EssayUK, essay.uk.com

15. Internet, Bulliet, Richard W., "Imperialism in the Middle East and North Africa", Encyclopedia of the Middle East and North Africa, 2004, The Gale Group, http://www.encyclopedia.com/doc/1G2-3424601324.html

16. Ritscher, Adam, "A Brief History of Afghanistan", Speech at Students Against War, Duluth, Minnesota

17. Ibid

18. Internet, Bulliet, Richard W., "Imperialism in the Middle East and North Africa", Encyclopedia of the Middle East and North Africa, 2004, The Gale Group,
    http://www.encyclopedia.com/doc/1G2-3424601324.html

19. Ibid

20. Ritscher, Adam, "A Brief History of Afghanistan", Speech at Students Against War, Duluth, Minnesota

21. Ibid

22. Internet, "World War 1: 100 Years Later, the True Story of Lawrence of Arabia, Smithsonianmag.com/history/true-story-lawrence-arabia-180951857/?no-is

23. Christianson, Scott, "The Origins of the World War 1 Agreement That Carved Up the Middle East: How Great Britain and France Secretly Negotiated the Skyes-Picot Agreement", Smithsonian.com, November 16, 2015. This article is excerpted from Scott Christianson's "100 Documents That Changed The World"

24. Ibid

25. Bouakdarian, Mansour, "Great Britain iv. British Influence in Persia, 1900-1921", Encyclopedia Iranica, December 15, 2002

26. Internet, "History of Iran", Wikipedia, wikipedia.org

27. Internet, "Dreyfus Affair", Wikipedia, Wikipedia.org

28. Internet, Tristam, Pierre, "What is the Balfour Declaration", about news, www.middleeast.about.com

29. Internet, "Balfour Declaration", about education, history1900s.about.com

30. Internet, Tristam, Pierre, "What is the Balfour Declaration", about news, www.middleeast.about.com

31. Ibid

32. Internet, "The White Paper of 1939", Wikipedia, wikipedia.org

33. Internet, Tristam, Pierre, "The U. S. and the Middle East Since 1945", About News, http://middleeast.about.com/od/usmideastpolicy/a/me070909b.htm

34. Ibid

35. Ibid

36. MacRae, Peter, *Twenty-first Violent Conflict: The Insufficiency of International Law*, San Diego, Montezuma Press, 2005

37. Genocide Convention of 1948, Article II

38. Rome Statute of the International Criminal Court

39. Charter of the United Nations

40. Wright, Quincy. "National Security and International Police", American Journal of International Law, Vol. 37, No. 3, 500.

41. Cassese, Antonio, *International Law*, Oxford, Oxford University Press, 2001

42. Waltz, Kenneth "Political Structures", in Robert Keohane, ed., *Neorealism and Its Critics,* New York, Columbia University Press, 1986

43. Bull, Hedley, *The Anarchical Society,* New York, Columbia University Press, 1995

44. Vattel, E. de., "Introduction", *The Law of Nations*, Translated by the Carnegie Institute, 1916, Quoted in Hedley Bull, *The Anarchical Society*, New York, Columbia University Press, 1995

45. Cassese, Antonio, *International Law*, Oxford, Oxford University Press, 2001

46. Falk, Richard, *Human Rights Horizons: The Pursuit of Justice in a Global World*, New York, Routledge, 2000

47. Lahneman, William J., "Introduction", In William J. Lahneman (ed.), *Military Intervention:Cases in Context for the Twenty-First Century*, Lanham, MD: Rowman & Littlefield, xiii-xviii. 2004a

48. Ibid, 2004b

49. Glennon, Michael J., *Limits of Law, Prerogatives of Power*, New York, Palgrave, 2001. "Why the Security Council Failed", Foreign Affairs, 2003, (May/June): 16-35

50. Ibid

51. Falk, Richard, *Human Rights Horizons: The Pursuit of Justice in a Global World*, New York: Routledge, 2000. "Ends and Means: Defining a Just War." The Nation 273: 11-16, 2001

52. Internet, Glanville, Luke, "The Responsibility to Protect Beyond Borders", Human Rights Lew Review, Oxford Journals, oxfordjournals.org/contents/early/2012/01/23

53. Dr. Adams, Simon, "Libya and the Responsibility to Protect", Occasional Paper, Global Centre for the Responsibility to Protect, 2012

54. Ibid

55. Internet, Glanville, Luke, "The Responsibility to Protect Beyond Borders", Human Rights Lew Review, Oxford Journals, oxfordjournals.org/contents/early/2012/01/23

56. Dr. Adams, Simon, "Libya and the Responsibility to Protect", Occasional Paper, Global Centre for the Responsibility to Protect, 2012

57. Dorota Gierycz. "From Humanitarian Intervention to Responsibility to Protect.", *Criminal Justice Ethics* 2010: pp. 110–128

58. Dr. Adams, Simon, "Libya and the Responsibility to Protect", Occasional Paper, Global Centre for the Responsibility to Protect, 2012

59. Marjanovic, Marko (2011-04-04) Is Humanitarian War The Exception? Mises Institute

60. Scheffer, David J. "Towards a Modern Doctrine of Humanitarian Intervention." University of Toledo Law Review Vol 23. (1992): 253-274.

61. Alton Frye. 'Humanitarian Intervention: Crafting a Workable Doctrine.' New York: Council on Foreign Relations, 2000.

62. Dr. Adams, Simon, "Libya and the Responsibility to Protect", Occasional Paper, Global Centre for the Responsibility to Protect, 2012

63. Internet, O'Connell, Mary Ellen, "Self-Defense", Oxford Bibliographies, oxfordbibliographies.com, last modified Nov. 30, 2015

64. Bowett, Derek. *Self-Defence in International Law*. Manchester, UK: Manchester University Press, 1958

65 Alexandrov, Stanimir. *Self-Defense against the Use of Force in International Law*. The Hague: Kluwer Law International, 1996.

66. Brownlie, Ian. *International Law and the Use of Force by States*. Oxford: Clarendon, 1963

67. "World Summit Outcome 2005", United Nations Review of Charter and Operations

68. Byers, Michael, and Simon Chesterman. 2003. "Changing the Rules About Rules? Unilateral Humanitarian Intervention and the Future of International Law." In J. L. Holzgrefe and Robert O. Keohane (eds.), Humanitarian Intervention: Ethical, Legal and Political Dilemmas. Cambridge: Cambridge University Press, 177-203.

69. Schmitt, Michael, "Preemptive Strategies in International Law" Michigan Journal of International Law, Vol. 24:513

70. Ibid

71. Ibid

72. Shultz, Richard H., and Andreas Vogt. "The Real Intelligence Failure on 9/11 and the Case for a Doctrine of Striking First", In Russell Howard and Reid Sawyer (eds.), *Terrorism and Counterterrorism: Understanding the New Security Environment,* Guilford, CT, McGraw-Hill/Dushkin, 405-28. 2004

73. Cassese, Antonio, *International Law*, Oxford, Oxford University Press, 2001

74. Article 51, Charter of the United Nations

75. Stern, Jessica, *Terror in the Name of God: Why Religious Militants Kill*, New York, HarperCollins, 2003

76. Peters, Gretchen, *Seeds of Terror: How Heroin Is Bankrolling* the *Taliban and Al Qaeda*, New York, Thomas Dunne Books, St. Martin Press, 2009

77. International Committee of the Red Cross, "Basic Rules of the Geneva Conventions and Their Additional Protocols", ICRC Publications ref.0365, 1988

78. Internet, Yusufzai, Rahimullah, "Rise and Fall", "What Happened to al Qaeda?", BBC News, April 6, 2016, bbc.com/news

79. Ibid

80. Article 51, The Charter of the United Nations

81 Internet, Yusufzai, Rahimullah, "Rise and Fall", "What Happened to al Qaeda?", BBC News, April 6, 2016, bbc.com/news

82. Charter of the North Atlantic Treaty Organization

83. Internet, "Response to 9-11", history.com/topics/response-to-9-11

84. Ibid

85. United Nations Security Council, "Resolution 1386

86. Mazari, Shireen M., "NATO, Afghanistan and the Region", Institute of Political Studies

87. Smith, Ben and Throp, Anabella, "Legal Basis for the Invasion of Afghanistan", House of Commons Library, February 26, 2010

88. Internet, "Iraq", Nuclear Threat Initiative, www.nti.org/learn/countries/iraq

89. Internet, Global Security, "IAEA and Iraq Nuclear Weapons", www.globalsecurity.org

90. Internet, "Iraq", Nuclear Threat Initiative",

   www.nti.org/learn/countries/iraq

91. Mohamed ElBaradei, *The Age of Deception: Nuclear Diplomacy in Treacherous Times*, New York: Metropolitan Books, 2011, p. 31.

92. Internet, "Iraq", Nuclear Threat Initiative",

   www.nti.org/learn/countries/iraq

93. Mohamed ElBaradei, *The Age of Deception: Nuclear Diplomacy in Treacherous Times*, New York: Metropolitan Books, 2011, p. 34; Jeffrey T. Richelson, *Spying on the Bomb*, New York: Norton, 2007

94. Internet, "Iraq", Nuclear Threat Initiative",

   www.nti.org/learn/countries/iraq

95. Mohamed ElBaradei, *The Age of Deception: Nuclear Diplomacy in Treacherous Times*, New York: Metropolitan Books, 2011, p. 34; Jeffrey T. Richelson, *Spying on the Bomb*, New York: Norton, 2007, p. 469.

96. Internet, "Iraq", Nuclear Threat Initiative",

   www.nti.org/learn/countries/iraq

97. U.S. Department of Defense, "Proliferation: Threat and Response," January 2001, p. 40; Joseph Cirincione with Jon B. Wolfsthal and Miraiam Rajkumar, *Deadly Arsenals: Tracking Weapons of Mass Destruction*, (Washington, DC: Carnegie, 2005), pp. 273-275.

98. Internet, "United Nations Security Council and the Iraq War", Wikipedia.org/wiki/list_united nationssecuritycouncil_resolutions_concerning_iraq

99. The Commission on the Intelligence Capabilities of the United States Regarding Weapons of Mass Destruction, *Report to the President of the United States*, March 31, 2005, pp. 8-9.100. Ibid

100. Ibid

101. Ibid

102. Internet, "United Nations Security Council and the Iraq War", Wikipedia.org/wiki/list_united nationssecuritycouncil_resolutions_concerning_iraq

103. The Commission on the Intelligence Capabilities of the United States Regarding Weapons of Mass Destruction, *Report to the President of the United States*, March 31, 2005, pp. 8-9.

104. Ibid

105. Internet, "Iraq", Nuclear Threat Initiative",
www.nti.org/learn/countries/iraq,

106. Comprehensive Report of the Special Advisor to the DCI on Iraq's WMD, Central Intelligence Agency, No. 1, p. 24, September 30, 2004, www.cia.gov.

107. Internet, "Iraq", Nuclear Threat Initiative",
www.nti.org/learn/countries/iraq

108. Comprehensive Report of the Special Advisor to the DCI on Iraq's WMD, Central Intelligence Agency, No. 1, p. 24, September 30, 2004, www.cia.gov.

109. Internet, "Iraq", Nuclear Threat Initiative",
www.nti.org/learn/countries/iraq

110. Comprehensive Report of the Special Advisor to the DCI on Iraq's WMD, Central Intelligence Agency, No. 1, p. 24, September 30, 2004, www.cia.gov.

111. Internet, "United Nations Security Council and the Iraq War", Wikipedia.org/wiki/list_united nationssecuritycouncil_resolutions_concerning_iraq

112. Internet, "Iraq", Nuclear Threat Initiative",
www.nti.org/learn/countries/iraq

113. The Commission on the Intelligence Capabilities of the United States Regarding Weapons of Mass Destruction, *Report to the President of the United States*, March 31, 2005, pp. 8-9.

114. Internet, "United Nations Security Council and the Iraq War", Wikipedia.org/wiki/list_united nationssecuritycouncil_resolutions_concerning_iraq

115. Ibid

ACKNOWLEGEMENTS

I would like to acknowledge two people who were extremely helpful in the production of this work. First, to my wife Pat, who tirelessly edited all my spelling, grammar and punctuation errors. She offered ideas for changes in phrasing or placement, most of which I agreed upon. Second, to my cousin Rod McCaskill, the computer whiz. Rod was responsible for the formatting and publication. His patience with this computer challenged author is remarkable. Every time I managed to cause the computer to "freeze" Rod walked me through the solution. To both of them my heartfelt thanks and love.

ABOUT THE AUTHOR

Peter MacRae holds a Master's Degree in Political Science from San Diego State University in San Diego, California. His area of special interest is in International Relations with an emphasis on the control of violent conflict.

Peter MacRae is the author of A *Measured Response: The United Global Security Partnership* and *The Poppies of Mohammed*. He has written numerous essays including: "Do We Have Cause to Fear Islam"; "Foreign Policy is an Inexact Science"and; "Why They Didn't Support Us", among others. His Master's Thesis, *Twenty-First Century Violent Conflict: The Insufficiency of International Law*, was published by Montezuma Press in 2005. Peter MacRae and his wife, Patricia "Pat", reside in the Wine Country of Northern California.

I SINCERELY HOPE YOU HAVE FOUND THIS INFORMATIVE.

NOW, PUT ON YOUR CRITICAL THINKING HAT AND FORM YOUR OWN OPINION.

PETER G. R. MAC RAE, M. A.

www.ingramcontent.com/pod-product-compliance
Lightning Source LLC
Chambersburg PA
CBHW081357280526
45788CB00009B/2913